IN THE
NATIONAL INTEREST

General Sir John Monash once exhorted a graduating class to 'equip yourself for life, not solely for your own benefit but for the benefit of the whole community'. At the university established in his name, we repeat this statement to our own graduating classes, to acknowledge how important it is that common or public good flows from education.

Universities spread and build on the knowledge they acquire through scholarship in many ways, well beyond the transmission of this learning through their education. It is a necessary part of a university's role to debate its findings, not only with other researchers and scholars, but also with the broader community in which it resides.

Publishing for the benefit of society is an important part of a university's commitment to free intellectual inquiry. A university provides civil space for such inquiry by its scholars, as well as for investigations by public intellectuals and expert practitioners.

This series, In the National Interest, embodies Monash University's mission to extend knowledge and encourage informed debate about matters of great significance to Australia's future.

Professor Margaret Gardner AC
President and Vice-Chancellor,
Monash University

SIMON WILKIE

THE DIGITAL REVOLUTION: A SURVIVAL GUIDE

MONASH
UNIVERSITY
PUBLISHING

Monash University Publishing
Matheson Library Annexe
40 Exhibition Walk
Monash University
Clayton, Victoria 3800, Australia
https://publishing.monash.edu

Monash University Publishing brings to the world publications which advance the best traditions of humane and enlightened thought.

ISBN: 9781922464217 (paperback)
ISBN: 9781922464231 (ebook)

Series: In the National Interest
Editor: Louise Adler
Project manager & copyeditor: Paul Smitz
Designer: Peter Long
Typesetter: Cannon Typesetting
Proofreader: Gillian Armitage
Printed in Australia by Ligare Book Printers

A catalogue record for this book is available from the National Library of Australia.

The paper this book is printed on is in accordance with the standards of the Forest Stewardship Council®. The FSC® promotes environmentally responsible, socially beneficial and economically viable management of the world's forests.

To my parents, Elizabeth and John.

PREFACE

The year 2020 went down as a watershed in which we saw a radical change in the economy. Contactless trade meant that cash all but disappeared, bricks-and-mortar retailers were under threat, the nature of work shifted, universities pivoted to online learning, and even a visit to the GP could be done over the internet. The world was already changing at what to many seemed a lightning-quick pace prior to the arrival of COVID-19, but the global pandemic accelerated the shift, compressing years of technological change into months. The result is that the world of early 2020 has been left behind as we race towards a digital future—a future driven by data collected at an ever-increasing rate.

Data is the new gold, and a modern-day gold rush means we are collecting phenomenal amounts of it through billions of devices connected to the internet. In 2003, a University of Pennsylvania professor, Mark Liberman, calculated that every word ever spoken up to that point in time could be captured in 42 zettabytes of data. Current widely quoted estimates are that, over the past year alone, we generated 44 zettabytes of data from the staggering thirty-four billion devices making up the much talked about Internet of Things. Put in another context, a zettabyte is equivalent to 1 000 000 000 000 of the more familiar gigabytes that make up the standard measure of memory in today's mobile phones and computers.

The impact of this transformation, described by World Economic Forum founder Klaus Schwab as the fourth industrial revolution, will be profound for the Australian economy and businesses. Old jobs will be destroyed even as new jobs are created, and companies will need to change the way they operate to become leaner and flatter. Governments will need to adopt new strategies to successfully navigate the transition to a digital economy and allow us to retain our standard of living and high levels of social welfare.

Drawing on my experience at Microsoft, other technology companies, and Monash Business School in Melbourne, my goal here is to unpack the nature of this digital disruption, the technologies enabling it, and what it means for work, business, government and other organisations. But my basic message is simple: we need to act—and act quickly—to develop our digital capabilities or we risk some grim consequences. Failure to do so could see Australia drop back to the status of a Third World economy as other, more visionary countries overtake us.

THE DIGITAL REVOLUTION: A SURVIVAL GUIDE

The concept of a fourth industrial revolution was minted by Klaus Schwab in his 2016 book of the same name.[1] He was describing the era following the computer revolution of the late twentieth century—the third industrial revolution—which he argued involved the 'democratisation' of information as the number of people with access to computers and the internet exploded. Information that had been hard to find and was the domain of a privileged few became accessible to all through search engines such as Google and the availability of increasingly powerful computers. This made it easier to make informed decisions, but it still amounted to access to information rather than to intelligence and expertise. People were still making the decisions.

The fourth industrial revolution now sweeping Australia is seeing a move from the realm of simply providing information to one of artificial intelligence (AI). AI refers to the ability of a computer or robot to perform tasks normally associated with intelligent humans or animals. The device does this through software that allows it to perceive and learn from its experiences, enabling it to better perform tasks and solve problems. AI is capable of assessing vast amounts of data and making decisions based on that review. As more and more people gain access to new and emerging technologies, access to intelligence is also becoming democratised. The hundreds of thousands of workers forced by the coronavirus pandemic to join the federal government's JobSeeker program saw this if they used LinkedIn to apply for a job, or when they interacted with Centrelink. Algorithms can be used to scan and reject résumés, match user profiles to jobs, and calculate benefits without interaction with a decision-making human being. No part of the planet is going to be left untouched by these sorts of changes.

An example of this democratisation of intelligence that pulls together all the technology pieces is a Microsoft project on which I worked in 2015. Project Kgolagano was centred on remote parts of Botswana and involved the unforeseen impact of the George W Bush administration's well-intentioned move to provide a human immunodeficiency virus (HIV) vaccine to African countries. It turned out there was a strong correlation between HIV and infections of human papillomavirus (HPV), a cause of cervical cancer. This produced a huge outbreak of cervical cancer in women in remote African locations where there were no diagnostics.

We worked with the University of Pennsylvania Medical School to use a technology called TV white space to introduce expanded wi-fi over unused television channels, producing a 10-kilometre-radius hotspot from an old-fashioned TV antenna. This enabled us to connect remote southern African schools and medical clinics to the internet, in turn allowing nurses to send medical imagery to the University of Pennsylvania's database, where it could be scanned by machine intelligence to determine whether cancer was present. It meant that somebody in the bush in Botswana had access to the best diagnostics in the world, thanks to AI, cloud computing, the telecoms revolution and the global internet.

Closer to home is a Monash University project. 'Jeffrey' is an online butler created by Monash students which acts as a 'study buddy' by combining Microsoft natural language processing with Amazon cloud computing. It essentially reads all classes and course information and reminds individuals what lectures they need to attend, when assignments are due, and which tutorials are coming up.

The first three industrial revolutions deeply affected society and, as I will show through a series of examples, the fourth is already doing the same. The first revolution involved technology primarily built on James Watt's steam engine and lasted from 1775 to 1885. It is seen as a 'deskilling' era in which many technological improvements replaced artisans with lower-skilled workers and machines.

The second industrial revolution, which spanned the end of the nineteenth century and the beginning of the twentieth, encouraged skill acquisition as a wealth of new technologies emerged, including the motorised assembly line and electricity. It was an era that encouraged acquisition, created the middle class, reduced inequality, and spread wealth more broadly. That trend stopped in about 1980 as inequality began to increase and skill acquisition began to level off. Machines again substituted for human skills—a classic example was the arrival of the electronic cash register, which meant operators no longer needed to be good at maths.

The third revolution was characterised by flat wages for the bottom 60 per cent of earners; a widening skill gap, with a premium placed on university graduates; and increasing underemployment.

The question now is what will the complex and sometimes unsettling fourth revolution bring, and what role will Australia play in it?

THE TECHNOLOGY PUSHING CHANGE

The lead-in to the first episode of the 1960s US television show *The Invaders* asked: 'How does a nightmare begin?' For Monash Business School, the answer was COVID-19, which in mid-March 2020 prompted the Australian Government to ban foreign arrivals and left 3000 of the school's 15 000 students stranded overseas. Worse was to follow as Victoria went into an initial coronavirus lockdown, emerging only to then be locked down for a second time. The dire situation prompted us to move 400 classes online and modify how we taught.

The process was not easy. We changed the way we assessed students three times as we adjusted our operations, even as we questioned the organisational structures, reporting practices and work culture. Yet there were unexpected advantages as technology produced a stream of new data on student engagement and interaction. Among other things, it allowed us to identify what worked best and what had failed. It also offered us the ability to experiment in ways previously unavailable to us.

One example involved the ability to know who turns up to lectures. Under normal circumstances, a lecturer does not know who is present, and they have little usable feedback on engagement. The new data stream allowed us to see which students logged into lectures, and we set up a discussion board around the presentations that revealed the questions students were asking each other. This gave us real-time feedback that indicated when things went wrong, and let us identify and contact students who were not engaged and might have been at risk of failure or dropping out. In short, the technology helped us to improve the quality of the education being provided.

This was just one of many new digital scenarios as people took to online meeting platforms, replaced physical conferences with webinars, attended virtual gym sessions, and tele-commuted from home. Many small businesses responded by switching to online sales, while bigger retailers ramped up their internet presence. There may have been a toilet paper shortage, but what was available could be ordered online and delivered to a person's door.

As far-reaching as these changes may seem, however, they are only a hint of the transformation of the global economy. The new combination of hardware, software and biology of the fourth industrial revolution is a quantum leap forward from the 'digital' third industrial revolution that saw the emergence of computers. It involves new products, services, company processes and business models which are riding a wave of innovative technologies.

Inexpensive devices such as cameras and sensors can now be connected to the internet to monitor everything from car performance to the way passengers move through airports. The data captured by this Internet of Things, or IoT—a term coined by sensor expert Kevin Ashton to describe how radio frequency ID chips used in consumer goods giant Procter & Gamble's supply chain could be linked to the internet—can be sent by new, faster wireless technologies such as 5G and stored cheaply on servers that can be combined to provide yet another important phenomenon: cloud computing. Most people are familiar with cloud computing through services such as Apple's iCloud and Microsoft's OneDrive, which allow you to store documents and other data outside your device, in an area that can be accessible to multiple people. This access allows collaboration and a much broader analysis and sharing of data than was previously possible.

Other technologies in the fourth wave are robotics; AI; biotechnology, such as genetic manipulation; and fully autonomous vehicles. Then there's nanotechnology, which focuses on materials on a molecular or atomic scale: a billionth of a metre. Examples include the extremely small particles used to make sunscreen more effective, and the billions of tiny transistors in computer microprocessors made by companies such as Intel. Yet another innovation is the 3D printer, which uses digital information from a computer to build a three-dimensional model. This allows components to be manu-factured quickly, on demand, in low volumes, and, when connected to the internet, wherever they're needed.

But the technology arguably creating the most discussion is machine learning. AI is made more powerful through the use of many computers distributed over the internet, and it can learn as it processes data. In some cases, it is surpassing human abilities in performing cognitive tasks such as translation, transcription and facial recognition. AI is now widely used in security applications and is making its way into settings such as airports, in applications ranging from biometrics to controlling the flow of passengers. It is already having an impact on the economic environment, the workplace and the public, and its influence is only set to get bigger.

An example we have already touched on is the way machine intelligence can quickly detect health threats and anomalies in X-rays and magnetic resonance imaging scans, by comparing them with big databases of past diagnoses. In regard to melanoma, one US system—SkinVision—can detect the condition with 95 per cent accuracy. Overall, AI increases the quality of health care and dramatically speeds up diagnostic processing, leading to the early identification of cancers and other health threats. The process can take as little as an inexpensive smartphone and access to the cloud, which means the technology can be affordably deployed to remote hospitals and clinics that would otherwise not have the necessary expertise.

Another area into which machine learning is making inroads is the online robot 'agent' known as a chatbot. When users of Microsoft Windows encounter an error message, they often seek to chat to a technician. But in many cases the technician is not a human being but a chatbot that has been trained on many thousands of human one-to-ones, to the point where it is generally more effective than an average human specialist at answering a user's question. Usually, the end user is not even aware that a machine is at the other end of the chat. Even if the chatbot does not understand what the user says, or detects an increasing level of frustration, it can 'escalate' the conversation to a human, along with a synopsis of the talk so far. Technicians can now focus on solving harder problems and spend a minimum amount of time on a scripted playbook of responses, while users are happier because they spend less time hanging on the phone waiting for someone—instead, they get a fast and accurate response. Chatbots can be cost-effectively introduced wherever a database of previous conversations exists, and they are cropping up across a variety of Australian industries such as airlines and online retailing.

A further illustration arises in how governments across Australia are keen to reduce the road toll, and how there is now technology that can help identify driver fatigue, thereby diminishing the number of accidents and cutting insurance premiums. Online emotion detection through camera images, which can tell when a driver is tired, is now reliable enough to be similar to human capabilities. For those of us who don't want a camera pointed at us in a car, fatigue can also be identified through the behaviour often exhibited by tired drivers, such as slamming on the brakes or swerving abruptly. Modern cars also monitor factors such as speed (including whether you're over the speed limit), how hard you brake, how hard you turn and how far you drive. It is possible for cars to detect that their drivers are not alert enough through this indirect observational data and then suggest they pull over.

An inexpensive device that plugs into your vehicle and stores the aforementioned data can send it to an insurance company when the car connects to your wi-fi back at home. A logical next step is for insurance premiums to be reduced for drivers who agree to install this device and who avoid fatigue and other offences such as speeding. Indeed, this is already happening—today in the United Kingdom, there are 750 000 car insurance contracts that are contingent on monitoring the data generated by a car.

There are other instances where conditions that cannot be observed directly can be inferred by looking at data, and many of these might also be used for contracts or special offers. Sticking with cars, modern vehicles register that a battery is about to die some two weeks before it stops working. Instead of driving until the battery is dead and then calling for help, it is now possible for drivers to connect their cars to wi-fi so that a text will be sent alerting them to poor battery health, while simultaneously offering a discount if they head to a service centre. This saves the road-side assistance provider time and money while also benefiting the driver.

It costs just US$1.25 to put a wi-fi chip in a car and, as the electric car manufacturer Tesla discovered, there can be huge advantages. When the Tesla 3 was given a 'not recommended' rating by the influential publication *Consumer Reports* because of poor-performing brakes, the company was able to send a software update to its wi-fi–enabled cars to fix the issue and change the rating.

Agriculture, a key export industry for Australia, is another area that can benefit from the fourth industrial revolution. Experiments have shown that farmers can reap efficiency gains and reduce environmental harm by deploying sensors at ground level or using overflights by drones or balloons to give a richer view of their fields. This allows them to cut costs by reducing water and fertiliser use while limiting environmentally damaging run-off. The use of pesticides can also be reduced to a tiny fraction of current levels, with the chemicals applied only when and where insect or weed activity is occurring.

Even criminals can expect to find it harder to ply their nefarious trade in the modern era. One parking garage in Burbank, California has twenty-two security cameras. The feeds from these cameras are shown on a screen which alternates between sixteen of them and the remaining six. A television screen has been placed next to the camera feed, so that the attention of attendants is drawn in the general direction of the security feeds, though not directly to them. Frequently, no-one is watching the feeds, but that doesn't matter because there is software to process them in real time, identify what's happening, and flash an alert whenever someone appears to attempt to open a car without a key or with a pry bar. Indeed, it is now feasible to automate the process of texting an alert whenever the person who gets in a car is not the person who parked it. As cameras get cheaper, we will use millions of them to secure our businesses, alerting human watchers when anomalies are detected, until eventually the process of dispatching security personnel is automated.

And how about a future where machines design workplace teams to solve problems or put together people to streamline workflows? Currently, this is often a random exercise whereby people meet at functions such as dinners and team-building exercises, find common ground, and end up collaborating. By mining the wealth of information to be found inside a company, such as email topics, machine intelligence is reaching the point where it can identify common interests and suggest meetings on specific issues. Microsoft's Delve already can suggest useful documents from across a company, providing a glimmer of what is possible as human capabilities are understood via machine learning applied to emails and other electronic records, and hardcopy documents.

None of these examples are that futuristic, which suggests profound changes spreading across many, even most, contemporary industries.

Such technology will alter the role of humans in the economy and will likely be as disruptive as the changes during the second industrial revolution, when mass-produced cars, aircraft, radio, telephones, electric lights, recorded music and cinema arrived simultaneously. The result back then was a mass movement of farmers to the city, and we can expect similar upheavals in the modern era: the technology trend firm Gartner predicts that 65 per cent of knowledge workers' career paths will be disrupted by smart machines.

Another motivation for Australian governments to make sure the nation is not left behind in all this is the tremendous impact of technology stocks on global markets, something that has been accelerated by COVID-19. Valuations for the big information, communications and technology companies have soared in recent times. Apple reached an astounding US$2 trillion on 20 August 2020, an amount roughly the size of Australia's superannuation balance.[2] Amazon, Microsoft and

Google have also all crashed through the once unthinkable trillion-dollar valuation. Australia may have so far managed to provide its citizens with a decent standard of living through mining and other primary industries, but the influence of these sectors is set to wane in comparison to surging tech companies. Wages as a percentage of gross domestic product in Australia have declined from almost two-thirds in 1975 to below 50 per cent today, and there is no indication that the trend will reverse, not without an influx of high-paying jobs bolstered by innovative new companies.

MARKET GAME CHANGERS

Markets have been around since the dawn of history, evolving along with our increasingly complex civilisations. There will be an uptick in this transformation as technology dramatically affects how and where many Australians work, how goods and services are priced, and how organisations and companies function.

The office is already changing as both businesses and workers see the advantages of telecommuting, and this is just the beginning of significant changes to the way we work. We can expect new measurements to become available through technology, and AI in particular, that will provide a clearer picture of worker output and workloads, leading to new organisational structures and ways of compensating people. People will switch jobs more often as the level of outsourcing and contracting increases.

How governments approach markets will also change as a wealth of data enables them to build models of economic activity based on disparate measures such as housing starts (privately owned new houses where construction has begun), traffic flows and energy usage. Australian companies will gain a much clearer idea of their customer bases, as well as how to set prices and the best way of venturing into new markets. Some of those new markets, such as those opened by the transportation operator Uber and the accommodation site Airbnb, have already been embraced enthusiastically by consumers.

Underlining Uber's popularity is the fact that it represents two distinct innovations in regard to the taxi industry. First, it took some friction out of the transportation booking process by devising an app that customers can use to call for a ride, and to see where the vehicle is and when it will arrive. In addition, having a credit card already on file has dispensed with tips and change, so that customers can quickly get on their way once they've arrived at their destination.

Serving customers well is an important business principle, but it is neither new nor revolutionary. The US department store pioneers John Wanamaker and Marshall Field were famous more than a century ago for their emphasis on customer service. The real innovation brought by

Uber was to re-envision the transportation business as a market. Instead of a company that's in the business of supplying taxis, Uber sees itself as a market-maker. It is in the business of connecting suppliers (drivers) and buyers (riders). Uber turned its business from a centralised model into a decentralised—though still organised—market.

This is important to understand. While businesses can be brought down by someone offering a better product or service at a better price, markets are much harder to disrupt. An entrant offering a competing marketplace must attract buyers to bring in sellers and sellers to bring in buyers. It is particularly challenging for an entrant to take on an incumbent in these circumstances. Indeed, the US website Craigslist, arguably a highly flawed market initially based on simply putting online traditional classified advertising without protecting user information, survived all challengers to demonstrate that even a dysfunctional market can resist disruption.

Future entrepreneurs would do well to recognise that a well-designed market is robust and often immune to challenges.

That doesn't mean, however, that new markets cannot be created where old ones already exist. Companies such as Amazon and Uber, for example, are trying to create a new freight market to provide customers with a smoother, simplified experience. This had already happened to some extent with the invention of standardised shipping containers, and the growth of global logistics giants such as FedEx, UPS and DHL. But friction remains in the system and Amazon and Uber are using distinct strategies to overcome this. Uber is using a more market-based approach with a service that allows businesses to find logistics providers much in the same way that Airbnb enables travellers to find accommodation. A similar take on this approach comes from the US online trucking website Convoy, which permits truckers to bid on loads across an expanding

North American network. Amazon, which is also a major supplier of cloud services, is leveraging its advantage of being both a large supplier and buyer in the marketplace, integrating freight as part of its overall package of services. Its subscription business, Amazon Prime, offers members free Australian domestic delivery and covers the cost of international freight for purchases above a certain amount, while offering other enticements such as movies, ebooks and music. All of this incentivises buyers to stick with its services while providing it with a treasure trove of data.

A classic lesson in how a company can define a new market involves the QWERTY keyboard. Towards the end of the nineteenth century, there were several competing keyboards, including the QWERTY layout invented by a Wisconsin newspaper editor to help telegraph operators transcribe Morse code. It didn't become a global standard because it was necessarily the best, but rather because of a canny move by gunsmiths

E. Remington and Sons. Remington provided QWERTY typing courses and cheap machines to secretarial schools. This meant that any company investing in what was then a costly typewriter had to buy one most typists could use, and the concept was locked in.

The digital transformation will enable Australian entrepreneurs to expand into business realms well beyond those we see now. While a market-based approach is not right for all businesses, those who make the transition can protect against disruption and even profit from the activities of others. A sharp illustration is provided by Apple's App Store, which from 2008 forged a market for apps and was able to take a 30 per cent cut of revenue from the companies that used it at a modest cost. At the same time, it created value for buyers by policing its store to prevent the introduction of malware (malicious software).

In Australia, electricity is a good candidate for a transition to a market using technology such as smart meters. Consumers are currently presented with a regulated electricity price and they are unlikely to drive home to turn off an air conditioner or refrigerator because of a rise in the cost of power. By using smarter devices, however, a consumer could allow some of their devices to be shut off when the price of electricity rises—experiments are already underway along these lines. Alternatively, they could use batteries to avoid buying power when prices are high.

This will all be increasingly valuable because of the nature of electricity. Unlike in other markets, it is critical in electricity provision to keep supply and demand balanced, otherwise transformers explode, or consumer appliances burn out. Historically, this was done by focusing almost entirely on supply. However, with the increasing use of renewables, the generation of which is out of the electric utility's control, the balancing of supply and demand will have to be performed in large part by consumers, with the requisite awareness of time-of-day or peak-load pricing. Fortunately, the digital transformation has arrived at just the right time to enable the practical market pricing of electricity.

THE PRICE IS RIGHT

Another big shift in Australia is being made possible by an improving ability to measure and analyse the behaviour of markets and people. One important aspect of this enhancement of market metrics will be an unprecedented ability to segment customers.

Segmenting customers and engaging in value-based pricing is an extraordinary money-maker for many companies because most of the revenue generated goes straight to the bottom line, and does so with little cost. Segments based on other purchases, geography, time of day or day of the week will combine with AI models of customers to approximate what the market will bear. We have already seen a crude version of this in Australia with supermarkets charging slightly higher prices in wealthy suburbs.

Today, it is rare to find a company that both manages prices across channels—the different ways in which companies sell products and services—and dynamically manages prices over time. Pharmaceutical firms are well known for managing channels effectively, while airlines dynamically manage pricing quite well. Yet this problem of successfully handling both is well within the reach of machine learning. Until now, the primary impediment has been data: knowledge of whether we see the same customer at different channels and at different points in time.

Finally, as better measurements enable companies to rely more on markets, for workers as well as other inputs, they will depend more on market pricing mechanisms such as auctions or bidding. We see this already in the crowdsourcing of design work like logos, but the competitive pricing of many other inputs should become much more prevalent.

THE VALUE OF GETTING MARKET DESIGN RIGHT

Many markets evolve organically because of a clever move by a company, but sometimes they can be purposefully designed. More Australian companies will take this path in the era of the new industrial revolution.

Market design is sometimes described as 'economics practised as an engineering discipline', in that it bears the same relationship to academic economics as mechanical engineering bears to physics. It is an applied discipline, respectful of theory but grounded in experimental observation, and it has resulted in at least four Nobel prizes. Just like a bridge which has not been engineered properly is likely to collapse, so too a market that has been badly designed is likely to suffer a similar fate. Also like mechanical engineering, market designers use a variety of tools to work their craft: economic theory, experiments, psychology, statistics and, lately, machine learning.

The basic idea is to tweak the rules of the game to affect the outcome, which necessitates a change in perspective by companies. Those in the business of operating markets and aspiring to follow the likes of eBay, Uber, Gumtree or Airbnb need to view themselves as the 'government' of their markets. This means they must take on all the traditional responsibilities of government: infrastructure, policing, court adjudication, taxes and subsidies, contract enforcement, the provision of a medium of exchange, and education. Market design also requires participants to have the information needed to make good decisions and to effectively manage incentives, so that participants take the desired actions.

Let's look at some applications of the discipline that can provide guidance for Australian organisations.

Market design made a global splash when it was used to guide the 1994 US Federal Communications Commission (FCC) spectrum auctions, and the resulting designs were then copied around the world. The FCC events use a 'simultaneous ascending auction', which means that many things are for sale simultaneously and bidders may substitute across items. Activity constraints force bidders to participate rather than take a 'wait and see' approach, which would lead to a stalling of the sale—as it did when Australia conducted its first spectrum auction in the mid-1990s. Licences worth more than US$100 billion have been sold through this innovative mechanism.[3]

Doctors in the United States (the United Kingdom has a similar program) are matched to hospital residencies through the National Resident Matching Program (NRMP), a large, computer-based initiative that represents a complex market mechanism. Here, physicians rank the hospitals they would like to work in, and hospitals rank the physicians they would like to employ. These rankings are entered into the NRMP, which then spits out a matching that has been carefully crafted so that everyone accepts the recommendations and there are no mutually beneficial side deals. The success of this matching program in large part accounts for US academic Alvin Roth winning the Nobel prize for economic science in 2012, and it has endured, having matched up to 20 000 physicians annually for decades.

The use in Yahoo and Google's advertising auctions of second-pricing—where bidders pay the second-highest bid rather than their own bid—also arose from market design. These auctions, which account for returns of over US$60 billion annually, have been the subject of intense market design optimisation that has produced substantial increases in revenue. An advertising auction is a market because it matches buyers (advertisers or their agents) with sellers (publishers with space for ads). While much of the inventory may come from a single publisher (a search engine), all of the search engines have partners on whose sites they also run ads.

An interesting market design conceptualised by University of Southern California Professor Milind Tambe and his colleagues shows that even areas such as security can benefit from this discipline.[4] When defending a target such as an airport, it is important that the security forces not be predictable. Predictable means exploitable—it makes it easy for attackers to go where the security forces are at their weakest. Moreover, it is impor-tant to place additional resources more often with the most attractive targets. However, people tend to fall into patterns and are not very good at randomising, particularly in a systematic way, so that the odds of defending more valuable targets are higher than the odds of defending those which are less valuable. Tambe's system uses centralised randomisation based on the attractiveness of the targets, and it communicates with the security force via a smartphone app. Even if a phone is compromised, this does not allow the attackers to know what the other forces are doing. This system has been in use at Los Angeles International Airport for over six years and has recently been deployed to counter poaching in Uganda, where it doubled the number of poachers caught in its first year of operation.

Market design is clearly an exciting, valuable field that has resulted in a set of technologies that can be used to create vibrant, efficient markets. Let's again consider the brilliant innovation of Apple's App Store.

Apple takes seriously its role as 'government' by attempting to eliminate malware and other malicious apps. However, when launched, the App Store was designed around the sale of apps.

The problem with the sale of apps is that it is hard for a better app to displace an existing one. If most people have already bought the incumbent's app, the entrant must be a lot better to shift it. So Apple set the terms of transfer as a rental, so that one bought the rights to, say, a year of the app. This makes it much easier to displace an incumbent—people will migrate at the time of renewal to the better app. To put it another way, the sale of apps encourages an investment in time to market, while the rental of apps encourages an investment in quality. It is a consequence of market design that there are a hundred thousand high-quality apps rather than, say, a million poor-quality apps.

Machine learning and access to new data in particular are pushing the frontiers of market design. For example, thousands of people die annually in stampedes and other forms of crushing in crowds. To limit this, video cameras are being used to assess the state of crowds, and in particular to identify dangerous situations. When problems are spotted, portions of the crowd can be shunted off to one side, or incoming people can be delayed by gates or even free gifts, or encouraged to take a different route. Indeed, the entire process of managing crowds can be handled by machines in this way, or they can be used to support human decision-makers.

Government policy is another area that can benefit. Traffic congestion, for instance, is incredibly costly—in many urban areas, workers spend around an hour per day experiencing traffic delays. The economic solution to this is to put a price on this congestion. Existing mechanisms price the use of roadways but typically not congestion, so that the pricing is not substantially higher in peak periods than during off-peak periods. It is a peculiarity of roads that the number of cars that can fit depends on congestion, and that if the crowding is high enough, adding more cars reduces the carrying capacity of the highways. In the transportation of liquids and gases in pipelines, injecting more into the pipes increases the amount that comes out. But with roads, once they are congested, injecting more cars reduces the number that come out per hour. Today, there is technology that can price congestion to maintain the maximum throughput and reduce the number of cars accessing the road in question.

Most analyses stop there, but just pricing some people out of a market is not always a good market design solution. The key in the example here is to use the revenue generated by pricing the roadways to subsidise alternative forms of transportation. In that way, what was otherwise an advantage only for rich people becomes an advantage for all, as the payments on the highways subsidise transport by train, tram or bus. In addition, the pricing of alternative transportation could be integrated to motivate people to move away from congested modes, encouraging the development of a vibrant and fast public transit system—one built on payments from the now congestion-free roadways.

These examples show that there are many situations in which market design can dramatically improve outcomes, especially when paired with new signals made available through the digital transformation. Many countries face the problem of removing subsidies without greatly harming the consumers who benefit from them, but a relatively straightforward solution would be to replace the subsidies on consumption with fixed payments based on past consumption and then reducing this over time. Designing procurement mechanisms to accommodate social goals like the participation of small business or domestic firms is a well-studied market design problem with off-the-shelf solutions. Balancing price and carbon emissions in electricity generation, optimising zoning for land use, auctioning emission permits, and the deployment of police forces are also problems that could benefit from a market design perspective.

CHANGING HOW WE VIEW JOBS

One implication of improved AI and metrics technology for Australian businesses is the likelihood that it will push employers towards signing up contractors rather than employing people directly. The move mirrors the impact on supply chains of the 1980s of enterprise resource planning software, which allowed companies to manage and integrate important parts of their business. The new technology gave firms an unprecedented level of insight into their physical goods and assets, and allowed them to 'lengthen' their supply chain by concentrating on core activities and outsourcing others. This better understanding of the sourcing of physical goods enabled companies to considerably tighten the supply process, sourcing through better planning and generally wringing improved efficiency from the process. In fact, it can be argued that the introduction of this software was a key enabling technology for the ensuing wave of globalisation.

Smarter and more diverse systems of measurement will now prompt companies to follow a similar process with their workers, substituting full-time employees for contractors on 'pay for performance' contracts. Companies will concentrate on their core capabilities and increase the use of outside specialists subject to better performance measurement. The type of insights that permitted goods to be sourced from further away and in a more agile fashion, reducing costs and improving quality, will now be applied to humans. The digital transformation will do this by processing workers' electronic records using machine learning, thereby outsourcing talent and making it possible to be much more nimble and effective in task assignment and team construction.

A major side effect of this is the ability of companies to restructure their operations much more quickly, so they will need to become adept at change management. Managers will need to be able to rapidly reassign employees by quickly identifying the needed skills and assigning the appropriate workers. It is a transformation that points to virtual teams, even virtual companies. Products can be rapidly prototyped, especially using 3D printers, then mass-produced and sold using scaled-up internet support. Overall, business processes will evolve at a much faster pace.

This nimbleness permits the creation of many new markets for specialised tasks which can be combined to produce value for customers. We can see the beginnings of this trend in companies such as Upwork. The New Jersey–based freelancing enterprise bills itself as the world's biggest remote talent platform, giving employers the opportunity to find talent across disciplines ranging from design, engineering and software development to writing and customer service. Employers can quickly generate shortlists of qualified experts in multiple disciplines around the globe using a proprietary AI matching technology. They can then view detailed profiles, portfolios, client reviews and ratings. Upwork argues that its technology allows employers to buy the exact services they need to get each project done quickly and efficiently.

Here is an example of how the ongoing improvement in metrics and AI can advance the effectiveness of contract labour, accelerating the trend of reducing full-time employees in favour of specialised, market-provided talent. This means that many specialised, human, task-oriented services will come into existence, and markets will be built on those.

To gain a concrete vision of this concept, consider the way a Hollywood movie is created. A movie might start with a draft script, and the studio then appoints a producer, director, screenwriter, actors, a key grip and so on. These people work together until the movie is made, at which point they disband. While some might be employees of the studio, many, even most, are not. The studio is primarily a vehicle for putting these resources together. This assembly is currently done using human intelligence and instinct, but as machines get better at understanding what works and what does not, such groups will increasingly be assigned by machine intelligence. This provides a model to complete complex tasks in other areas that are not yet valuable enough to warrant such specialised, market-based approaches.

Some of this involves the so-called 'gig economy', where people compete against other individuals for work, but it is likely that new, specialised firms will allow people to remain in traditional employee relationships despite the increased contracting of talent. However, it is also probable that more people will become self-employed, and that these changes will accelerate the long-term movement away from lifetime employment, opening up the need for discussions by society on labour laws as well as the scope and role of social safety nets. The trend towards outsourcing, when combined with the speed of disruption coming from AI and automation, will demand that people 'retool' more frequently to adjust to the dramatic changes facing them over their working careers.

The ability to measure people more closely may also change the way in which they are paid. Consider the use of smarter metrics in the compensation paid to a sales force. Each person has a sales target and their compensation depends on whether and by how much that target is exceeded. Complaints about sales targets are common, and they are the subject of intense lobbying, but the same system used to mine documents and emails could also suggest targets based on an analysis of the likelihood of success and the expected time that the best course of action will take. This would provide stronger incentives while being fairer overall.

Exactly how the digital transformation will play out in the workforce will depend on whether a technology complements a job or substitutes for it. A complement is a product that makes another product more valuable, such as a keyboard for a tablet computer, or a screen for a projector. Substitutes, on the other hand, reduce the value of a good, in the way that owning a PC reduces the value of a tablet computer, or owning a mobile phone reduces the value of a home phone.

What is not well known—in fact, the opposite is often asserted—is that there have been significant periods of time when technology has not been complementary to skill acquisition. As mentioned earlier, some call the first industrial revolution, with its technology primarily built on Watt's steam engine, the deskilling era. The cotton gin was a substitute for the relatively skilled activity of extracting seeds from cotton, so it reduced the need to acquire skills and lowered wages. Another example is the pin factory detailed in Adam Smith's 1776 book *The Wealth of Nations*. In a classic observation about the division of labour, Smith details how one man draws out the wire, another straightens it, a third cuts it, and a fourth points it, while others make the head and whiten it. None of them makes an entire pin. Of course, by contrast, the second industrial revolution greatly encouraged the acquisition of skills.

The question is whether the technologies now coming onstream complement or substitute for human skills. This is a hard call to make, but the classic science fiction vision of millions of people rendered unemployed by the rise of machines is unlikely to be correct.

The first thing to understand is that all technologies substitute for human labour. That fact does not matter in the long run, because there is an infinite number of things we would like done if the price is low enough. For example, a worker with a bulldozer can do the work of a hundred people with shovels, so a bulldozer substitutes for human labour. A bulldozer requires much greater skill to operate than a shovel does, so a bulldozer is also a complement to human skills, and the operator of the machine earns more than somebody wielding a shovel.

On the other hand, the cash register eliminated the need for cashiers to do maths and lowered their wages. And now supermarkets have self-service kiosks that reduce the need for cashiers, while radio frequency identification technology (RFID) is tipped to eliminate even this process with a system that automatically adds up and debits a bill as a shopper exits a store. RFID uses a small chip attached to an item that can be interrogated using an electromagnetic pulse from a reader and is often used to track inventory. The tag responds to the pulse by transmitting data to the reader, in this case an inventory number and a price.

Technologies that are likely to substitute for skills include machine intelligence, big data (very large and valuable datasets), programs that write software, driverless vehicles and industrial automation. We can see some of this in the Australian mining industry, where the introduction of robots as well as driverless trucks and trains is reducing the number of onsite jobs. Technologies that are likely to be complements include mobile computing devices, mobile payment systems, virtual reality, voice control, 3D printing and online markets. The jury is still out on which camp will claim developments such as the cloud, the IoT, drones and the freelance employment model.

The good news is that those technologies that complement skill acquisition tend to increase workers' wages. The technology may replace some workers, but increases in the abilities of the remaining workers see wages rise, because employers must pay for higher levels of skills. The result is that income inequality tends to fall. This may happen with a lag—the replacement of lots of workers with technology may mean that it takes some time for employment to return to its full level. But if the technology in question increases the need for skills in the economy, wages will be higher and income inequality less.

Only time will tell how all this plays out.

THE FUTURE OF THE FIRM

So how should Australian companies prepare for the many new challenges and opportunities arising at a pace that we have not experienced for more than a century?

While much has been written about the future of jobs, less attention has been paid to the future of the firm. Most people take the existence of firms for granted, but in a 1937 paper, the British economist Ronald Coase asked a profound question: if markets are so efficient at allocating, why do firms exist?[5] What he found was that firms and the command-and-control system we call management were better than individuals at dealing with several of the expenses incurred when buying or selling a good or service. These included costs such as identifying funding sources, gathering information, and negotiating agreements and ensuring all parties stick to them— what Coase called transaction costs. But he also noted that these transaction costs were the key determinants of the 'limit of the firm', the point at which companies stop growing.

What is the implication of this for modern firms, and what role is technology playing? In companies, management deals with transaction costs and accompanying issues such as moral hazard, or the risk that a party has not entered into a contract in good faith or is lying; and adverse selection, where sellers have information not available to buyers (or vice versa) about some aspect of a product's quality. Digital disruption and new torrents of data can be used to ameliorate these problems.

Indeed, this is already being done. Digital disruption challenges the limits of the firm and changes the calculus on the benefit of management and other organisational structures versus the cost. This means firms will become smaller, affording markets the ability to replace transaction and resource allocation decisions within the firm. In addition, companies will become 'flatter' as data-driven decision-making negates the need for management, and prompts mechanisms such as career paths to align incentives with behaviour.

One thing we often take for granted is that firms will be long-lived. Think about how Microsoft Corporation was founded in 1975 to produce a single product, MS-DOS, to solve a specific problem: namely, create an operating system for the new IBM PC. Forty-five years later, the same institution not only still exists, it is operating in vastly different markets, from Xbox gaming platforms to cloud computing. And in the process of doing so, it has generated enormous profits for its shareholders. But why is this an efficient allocation of resources across such a lengthy time span and different markets? That may not be the case in the future.

If we think about digital disruption as flattening an organisation and reducing the role of expertise, then the future of the firm is likely to look much more like the Hollywood model we visited previously than that of Microsoft. To recap, in Hollywood, a film is set up as a once-off production (two movies in a series are sometimes filmed back to back, but this is exceptional). The principals assemble the key talent, contracts specify the profit shares, and all the required skills are purchased through the market to produce the movie. The film is eventually released and its creators hope to make a profit, at which point the operation is dissolved. Any profits are then distributed to the producers and the talent through the contractual agreements and everyone moves on to their next venture.

The future firm—or some new organisational form—is likely to be modelled on this. Someone identifies a problem that, if resolved, could generate profit, and they determine the set of skills needed to come up with a solution. They go to platforms such as GitHub and Seek to identify talent, form a venture to solve the problem, sell the venture to a larger platform so that they can monetise it, carve up the profit, and then turn their attention to a new opportunity. Indeed, much of the economy in California is already operating in this way. In the last two decades, the leading mode of 'exit' for start-ups has become acquisition rather than an initial public offering of shares—most of these acquisitions have been undertaken by the tech giants.

Getting back to the question of what Australian firms need to do, I have several suggestions.

First, embrace artificial intelligence. Gartner suggests that many of the components of AI are at the top of its 'hype cycle' right now. Gartner uses the hype cycle to graphically represent the way technologies are adopted, starting from a trigger point and moving through a 'peak of inflated expectations' and 'a trough of disillusionment' to a 'plateau of productivity'. With AI at the top of the inflated expectations cycle, we can expect a period of rampant pessimism about the technology. Yet AI has already begun to solve formerly intractable problems, and so it will transform business processes. The key is to identify how to leverage this early and optimally redeploy human talent.

A nice example of this involves court reporters. About twenty years ago, the automatic transcription of courtroom testimony became available. Court reporters could have competed with this technology, and that would have worked for a while, because courts are typically slow to accept such developments. Instead, court reporters repositioned themselves as the people who produce accurate transcripts, starting with the automated version. That is, the AI now works for the reporter instead of competing with the reporter. This insured the continued relevance of court reporters even as the transcription technology improved.

Generally, both workers and companies should embrace AI by acquiring the skills needed to use it as a tool. This is the best way not to be replaced by the technology.

Second, emphasise human productivity. Human capital—the skills of the workforce—represents about half of the value of the average corporation, with the balance of the value split between physical goods and intangibles (intellectual property, goodwill, patents and so on). As human capital is the single largest source of value in companies, improving it is the quickest and most sustainable route to increasing company value. Data on the digital lives of employees is going to prove immensely valuable in understanding and optimising this asset.

Third, develop nimble teams. The big dividend from better understanding a workforce is rapid redeployment. This will require a mindset shift as well as the leveraging of technology, but the ability to dramatically reduce development cycles and time to market makes it worthwhile. As the human capital supply chain lengthens, nimble teams exploit new opportunities.

Fourth, develop new metrics. The sea of data already being stored by many companies contains many actionable insights, and provides the capacity to more accurately assess whether a given action is likely to lead to success in the long run. Some care must be taken to avoid 'vanity metrics', those that make you look good but don't help you to understand your performance in a way that benefits future strategies. But nonetheless, the potential for better, more fine-grained metrics, especially for customer satisfaction, is an important advantage.

Finally, while it is not always possible, keep an eye out for the opportunity to create a new market, either to replace an existing non-market institution or to create brand-new matches. Creating a market allows a firm to harness creative forces outside the organisation, as well as to generate sustainable profits in an environment where disruption is rampant and few incumbents are unchallenged by new business models.

A RISING CYBERSECURITY THREAT

An incredible one billion camera sensors are put into use each year. Some are part of the IoT, used for security, traffic monitoring and in industry, while others are in mobile phones and laptops. This remarkable growth speaks to the two issues that tend to dominate technology coverage in the general media: privacy and cybersecurity. This is not surprising given the actions of various states, fears about the influence of social media, and arguments about how the big corporations such as Google and Facebook use our data.

Organised crime has also been quick to jump on the technology bandwagon, with the 'dark web' evolving in recent times from a largely unknown underground term to a fact of life. The dark web is an encrypted part of the internet that cannot be accessed by normal browsers and is not indexed by search engines. It is a marketplace for stolen personal details, drugs, and other unsavoury items such as child pornography. Enforcement agencies such as the US Federal Bureau of Investigation and the Australian Federal Police monitor the dark web and have launched successful prosecutions.

There is an economic cost to all this. The Australian Competition and Consumer Commission (ACCC) estimates that in 2019, Australians lost $634 million to scams, and that there were 353 000 reports made that year to its own Scamwatch website, other government agencies and the nation's big four banks. Heading the losses were compromised business email scams costing $132 million, investment scams amounting to $126 million and romance scams costing $83 million. The consumer watchdog estimates that Australian businesses and individuals lost a staggering $2.5 billion in the decade to 2019—but it concedes that that number is probably vastly understated. As ACCC deputy chair Delia Rickard notes, modern cons are now taking advantage of social media, apps and new payment methods.[6]

While technology is the vehicle scammers use to obtain their ill-gotten gains, most scams do not involve hacking. Ninety per cent of online intrusions comprise what is called 'a legitimate entry', where a scammer obtains somebody's ID and password. Still, an increase in activity by state agencies and criminal groups has seen a rise in the number of high-profile hacks suffered globally by big companies and government agencies, including in Australia.

On the plus side, all clouds, even those of the internet, have a silver lining. An economic consequence of the lost money, reputational damage and security concerns stemming from disreputable online activity will be a dramatic growth in cybersecurity jobs. The federal government is already moving to address the increasing threat, particularly from state-backed hackers, having poured $1.3 billion into cybersecurity in 2020 to hire 500 additional experts. According to the employment website Seek, security job ads in the information and communications technology industry grew by almost 25 per cent in 2019.[7]

Meanwhile, the leading cybersecurity professional organisation (ISC)² estimates that the global cybersecurity workforce gap in 2019 was more than four million, and that the workforce of 2.8 million in the eleven economies it covers needs to grow by 145 per cent to meet the demand for skilled talent. Its best estimate is that Australia in 2019 already supported a cybersecurity workforce of 107 000 and that we can only expect the demand for these important workers to grow.[8] This is being partly driven by the prodigious growth of the IoT, including those billion additional cameras a year, and the difficult question of how we will secure this galaxy of devices.

Like charity, however, cybersecurity begins at home. It is crucial that Australian businesses give this issue the necessary attention and funding. There is no shortage of horror stories about companies that have lived to rue the day they let their security slide. One classic anecdote involves a US hospital that failed to update from Windows 7 to the much more secure Windows 10, even though the latter was free. North Korean hackers used a backdoor in the earlier Windows program, which at the time was no longer supported by Microsoft, and gained access to sensitive medical records.

This raises the question of whether there should be some rules around liability to ensure companies undertake the required upgrades in an appropriate time frame. Individuals also need to constantly upgrade their operating systems and security as part of the vigilance needed to tackle online threats.

THE PROBLEM OF PRIVACY

It may not be immediately evident in the way everyone signs away their data to Google and Facebook, but people and organisations value privacy. We know this because of a study conducted by Microsoft after Edward Snowden in 2013 revealed that big US tech and telecommunications companies had breached privacy laws by getting into bed with the National Security

Agency (NSA)—the NSA was getting metadata from international phone calls, had tapped into submarine cables, and was receiving information from countries in the Five Eyes intelligence-sharing alliance. Microsoft looked at the growth rates of the US firms implicated in the NSA privacy breach and compared them with those of the international firms that were not implicated. What it found was that the breach slowed the growth of the US firms, basically costing them a combined US$30 billion. That confirms that people value privacy.

In addition, the adoption of cloud computing—the fastest-growing and arguably most important industry in the world, which is highly dependent on security because of the data it stores—slowed for about six months. Then a price war saw charges fall about 65 per cent in a year and demand subsequently pick up again.

Many tech companies are also becoming more serious about protecting privacy, even as an explosion of new devices around the home and workplace sees more and more data being hoovered up. Governments are trying to address the issue too, but often from different perspectives. A number of jurisdictions have introduced online privacy provisions, including the European Union (EU), New Zealand, India, Sweden and the United Kingdom. The United States, on the other hand, has left it up to industry to police itself, unless there is some involvement by a foreign entity.

In regard to Australia, the 2019 report of the ACCC's Digital Platforms Inquiry found deficiencies in domestic law when it came to the dominance of the leading digital platforms and their impact across the country's economy, media and society.[9] The inquiry produced twenty-three recommendations covering issues such as the market power of Google and Facebook and the spread of disinformation. From a privacy viewpoint, it found that consumers were not adequately informed about how their data was collected or used, and had little control over the huge range of information being gathered. The targeted recommendations included privacy law reform, the introduction of a code of practice aimed at digital platforms, and redress for serious invasions of privacy. The commission was also worried that long, complex privacy policies offered consumers the illusion of control but instead gave platforms broad discretion concerning how they would use data.

The ACCC set up a specialist Digital Platforms Branch and in September 2020 released the first of a series of biannual Digital Platform Services Inquiry interim reports. The report again showed that many platforms were able to extensively track users' activities online and on mobile apps using cookies, software development kits and other technologies.[10]

Australia remains in the international spotlight over its draft News Media and Digital

Platforms Mandatory Bargaining Code, which is aimed at forcing big tech giants to pay local media organisations for the use of their articles. But the question of who owns personal data is likely to remain vexed. In 2016, the EU introduced the General Data Protection Regulation, which applies to the data of individuals located in the EU at the time the data was collected, and also applies to any international business with customers in the EU, including those in Australia. However, this concerns an informed consent doctrine and does not really change who owns the data.

Australians individually have no market power when it comes to dealing with tech firms, although one radical idea is to impose a digital advertising tax on platforms that monetise our data but give little in return. Little worth may be attached to the data relating to a single individual, but the value of that information adds up to a substantial sum across the entire community, and the government could collect that money on our behalf. A 10 per cent tax would raise billions in much the same way that we impose the Minerals Resource Rent Tax on mining companies, and it could be used to fund social programs.

EVOLVING EDUCATION

The rise of AI in the fourth industrial revolution means that education will no longer be 'won and done'—people will not go to school, get a tertiary education and then embark on a career. Instead, they will need to think about reskilling several times in their lives as AI becomes more influential in work, making some jobs redundant while creating others. A worker could attend an institute of Technical and Further Education at one point of their career or a university at another as they retrain for a new future. There will also need to be a new funding model—instead of the current Higher Education Contribution Scheme, we might need to give people a credit bank they can draw from over their lifetime.

This will all add up to a major cultural change, with people expecting to be in and out of the workforce over their lifetime, leaving it for retraining and reskilling. It will require a change in government policy as well. A change in the way firms think about their employees will also be needed, which is one area where market design could be applied.

Typically, workers seeking retraining first acquire new skills and then seek employment. From a market perspective, it is hugely advantageous to unify these two processes so that workers can acquire the skills relevant to a specific job rather than simply hoping that there will be an employer who wants the skills they have at the end of the education or training process. One design would attach government retraining funds to a worker, who could then take them to an employer. The worker would be apprenticed or retrained on the job as part of a well-thought-out design, which would also deter employers who take payments without providing useful training. This employer involvement is clearly advantageous to the worker, who avoids the uncertainty of searching for jobs; and to the employer, who is subsidised during the skill-acquisition period. Bringing employers into the market will make the market much more effective at both matching workers with employers, and matching workers with the skills they need to be employable.

In the shorter term, Australia must also address an urgent need for workers who are highly skilled in computer science, data science, business analytics and economics. Tech firms are so hungry for PhD talent that they acquire companies purely for their employees. Stanford University and University of California, Berkeley feed their PhDs straight to California's Silicon

Valley. In Boston, tech companies have literally set up across the street from the Massachusetts Institute of Technology to hire PhDs, while Microsoft has research labs next to Cambridge University in England and near Tsinghua University in Beijing. Amazon alone recently hired 140 PhD economists.

The key lesson is that tech goes to where the talent is. If Australia is to get a piece of the pie, we need to make some simple policy changes.

A return to Australia in 2019 after a 35-year career in the United States left me awestruck at the changes that had occurred in the local higher education sector, and it also left me in no doubt that we have several of the world's best universities, delivering top-notch research and skilled undergrads. However, I was also struck by the lack of the symbiotic relationships between tech and leading universities that are a feature of the US landscape. Australia is underperforming when judged according to world standards in turning out a critical mass of outstanding PhDs, and we desperately need to produce more in the key areas driving technological change.

This is not only about there being great jobs at stake. It's also about having a stake in the future. Compared with its peer nations, Australia underspends on research by about $5 billion a year. Moreover, the caps on funding for domestic students mean that about 300 000 Australians who will reach university age during the 2020s will be denied places in tertiary education. These huge problems, which will severely impact the level of research that is achieved, could be easily addressed by changing the funding criteria in the Research Training Program (RTP). This would require increasing the time in which PhDs are subsidised from four to five years, and removing the bias that encourages universities to play it safe by funding less-risky research.

The way funding is considered under the RTP also preferences decisions in favour of high-cost areas such as medicine, where the government subsidy is much more substantial compared with areas that have lower laboratory and material costs, including computer science, economics and data analytics. Finally, the RTP weights industry funding—but if the tech sector is not here, there will be little funding from industries of the future as Australia doubles down on the industries of the past.

Together, these criteria limit Australia's ability to develop talent in the key tech-sector disciplines. Yet Australians who have American PhDs have held senior economist or data scientist positions at companies like Amazon, Uber, Microsoft and Expedia. We have the talent—it's just that we export it. We need to nurture some home-grown talent and develop the domestic tech industry.

A proposal to augment the RTP with a new strategic fund would need to identify key strategic disciplines where Australia needs to bulk up in PhDs. It would then competitively award five-year PhD fellowships to our best students if they join an eligible program. Even if we started with a modest number, say 200 a year, this would help create critical mass in these key areas and prime the ecosystem. The additional cost would be minor, but the investment would offer a different future to Australia, one where we change our destiny by becoming a tech hub rather than a market.

THE DEATH OF CASH

Plastic now rules where cash was once king, and COVID-19 is accelerating that trend. The Reserve Bank's fifth survey of consumer payments, conducted in October and November 2019, before the pandemic struck, found that people were already gravitating towards cards.[11]

In 2007, 69 per cent of payments were made by cash, but this had dropped to 27 per cent by 2019. Card payments over the same period more than doubled to 63 per cent, with most of that increase coming from debit cards, which accounted for 44 per cent of payments in 2019. Payment methods that were not prevalent in 2007, such as internet banking and PayPal, collectively accounted for about 5 per cent of payments, while BPAY remained about the same at 2 per cent. Cheques had already lost popularity by 2007 and by 2019 they accounted for just 0.2 per cent of all payments. The Reserve Bank found the ease of 'tap and go' means that the shift away from cash is occurring even for the small transactions people may once have paid using their loose change. The number of direct debits has also doubled since 2013 to 9 per cent of total transactions.[12]

Some pundits are suggesting that Australia could become entirely dependent on non-cash payments as early as 2022. The change to a cashless society has obvious ramifications for the black economy and criminals, but it also gives financial institutions unprecedented access to data about the areas where people spend their money, which bears thinking about.

Electronic payments must also remain low-cost and secure, and consideration must be given to those members of the community who still rely heavily on cash, such as the elderly and the poor. The Australian Banking Association estimates there are still half a million bank customers, most aged over seventy, who actively use a passbook or transaction account with no linked debit card. This scenario proved to be a problem in Sweden, where a move to electronic systems so restricted the availability of currency that politicians were forced to pass laws requiring the nation's major banks to offer cash services.[13]

Other consequences include moves by banks to close branches and shut down costly automatic teller machines, something that has consequences for rural communities.

KEEPING UP IN A CHANGING WORLD

Australians lived well during the twentieth century on the back of primary industries, but times are changing. The present danger is that the economic rents from traditional sources such as mining, agriculture and construction, which have long sustained our lifestyle, will soon no longer be enough. Australia urgently needs to follow the money if it is to ride the fourth industrial revolution into a brighter future. And the money is where the tech firms are. Apple alone is worth multiples of the combined market capitalisation of Australia's biggest miners: BHP, Rio Tinto, Fortescue Metals and Newcrest Mining.

We are excellent miners, and this key segment of the economy will continue to underwrite our lifestyle for the near term, but its importance is destined to diminish. Climate change means the writing is already on the wall for coal, which adds $70 billion to the country's coffers through exports.[14] Our major customer, China, is moving to diversify its resource suppliers even as its spreading influence results in trade tensions. We must choose whether we want to continue to resemble a Third World country as the rest of the globe moves ahead of us, or join the surge.

If you talk to the big tech firms, you'll find that Australia is not on their radar when it comes to establishing research centres. They put them in Israel, they put them in China, in the United Kingdom. The US companies view Australia as a sales market. That must change, and the federal government has a crucial role to play in terms of education and training, research funding, and other support for the development of the tech industry.

The digital revolution will not be without its issues for workers, companies and the economy. There will be dislocation and inequality as the changes gather pace. Workers will need to retrain and change jobs several times during their career, the nature of firms will have to change too, and markets will need to evolve to match the new circumstances. But those changes are coming regardless. The question for Australia is: do we ride the new technological wave, or do we let it inundate us?

ACKNOWLEDGEMENTS

Thank you to Louise Adler for organising my contribution to this important new series, and for making sure we got there. Thanks also to Paul Smitz for his editing work and managing the project, in concert with Monash University Publishing. I would especially like to thank Steve Creedy for his exceptional research and word-smithing assistance in finalising this book.

NOTES

1   Klaus Schwab, *The Fourth Industrial Revolution,* World Economic Forum, Cologny, Switzerland, 2016.

2   Jack Nicas, 'Apple Reaches $2 Trillion, Punctuating Big Tech's Grip', *The New York Times,* 19 August 2020.

3   Ben Christopher, 'The Spectrum Auction: How Economists Saved the Day', *Priceonomics,* 19 August 2016.

4   Marc Ballon, 'A Safer World', *Viterbi Magazine,* spring 2015.

5   Ronald Coase, 'The Nature of the Firm', *Economica,* vol. 4, no. 16, 1937, pp. 386–405.

6   Australian Competition & Consumer Commission, 'Scams Cost Australians over $630 Million', press release, 22 June 2020.

7   Jade Macmillan, 'Cybersecurity Spending Gets $1.35 Billion Boost in Wake of Online Attacks against Australia', *ABC News,* 29 June 2020.

8   (ISC)^2, *Strategies for Building and Growing Strong Cybersecurity Teams,* (ISC)^2 Cybersecurity Workforce Study, Clearwater, FL, 2019.

9   Australian Competition & Consumer Commission, *Digital Platforms Inquiry: Final Report*, June 2019.

10 Australian Competition & Consumer Commission, *Digital Platform Services Inquiry: Interim Report*, September 2020.

11 James Caddy, Luc Delaney, Chay Fisher and Clare Noone, 'Consumer Payment Behaviour in Australia', Reserve Bank of Australia, 19 March 2020.

12 Ibid.

13 Maddy Savage, 'Sweden's Cashless Experiment: Is It Too Much Too Fast?', *NPR*, 11 February 2019.

14 Lucas Baird, 'Albanese Backs Australian Coal Exports', *Financial Review*, 17 January 2020.